New Puppy

by
Tammy Raden

AuthorHouse™
1663 Liberty Drive
Bloomington, IN 47403
www.authorhouse.com
Phone: 1-800-839-8640

First published by AuthorHouse 5/24/2010

ISBN: 978-1-4520-0797-7 (sc)

Library of Congress Control Number: 2010907209

Printed in the United States of America
Bloomington, Indiana

This book is printed on acid-free paper.

authorHOUSE®

To Colby, Alexie, and Zachary, who are the love of my life and the inspiration behind all my stories.

I rushed from my neighbor's house feeling great.
I had the best news, and it couldn't wait.
Their dog had puppies they were giving away.
I wanted to know if I could get one today.

So as fast as I could, I hurried home,
but Mom was talking on the phone.

I needed to make sure she understood
why owning a puppy would be very good.
So I thought it might be a smart thing to do
to come up with reasons why she'd think so too.

I could say that a puppy is a nice thing to own.
He can help keep us safe when he is all grown.

And when he gets older, we can play at the park.

He can sleep by my side when I'm afraid of the dark.

Having a puppy would be good for me
by teaching me responsibility.
I would walk him, feed him, and pick up his mess.
I promise at least I would do my best.

My puppy would be there if I got down,
to lick my face and run around.

The only thing my puppy will see
is that I love him and he loves me.

Yes, my puppy and I would grow to be
the very best friends there ever could be.

So when Mom finally finishes and says goodbye,
I had all my reasons. I was ready to try.

But instead I yelled in a single gasp,
"The puppies can leave their mom at last.
And I would feel so very lucky
if you would say I could have a puppy!"

That's all I said, and I don't know why.
Then I felt I was going to cry.

But Mom only looked and gave me a smile.
She said, "That was Dad and he'll be home in awhile."

Oh why did I blow it? What did I do?
All the reasons I thought up I knew were all true.
Now I was sure they would never agree
that owning a puppy was the best thing for me.

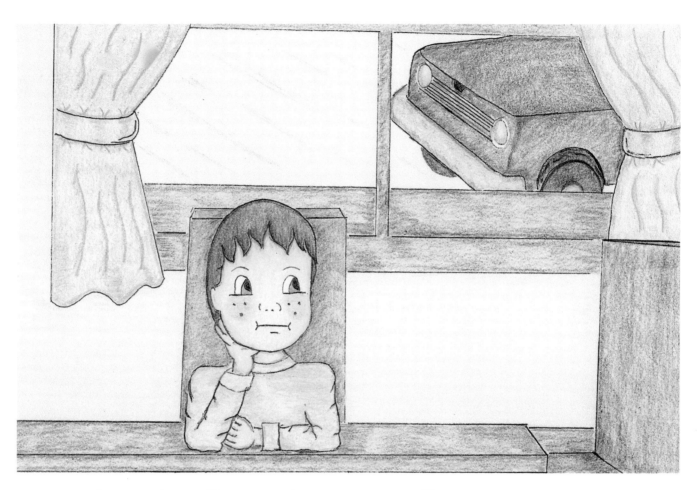

And while I was thinking that I should give up,
I heard my dad's car. He was just pulling up.

So I ran out to greet him, and what did I see?

Mom by his side and a puppy for me.

CPSIA information can be obtained
at www.ICGtesting.com
Printed in the USA
LVIC06n1921110117
520642LV00009B/34

9 781452 007977